Stress Relieving
YOGA RETREAT
Yoga Coloring Book

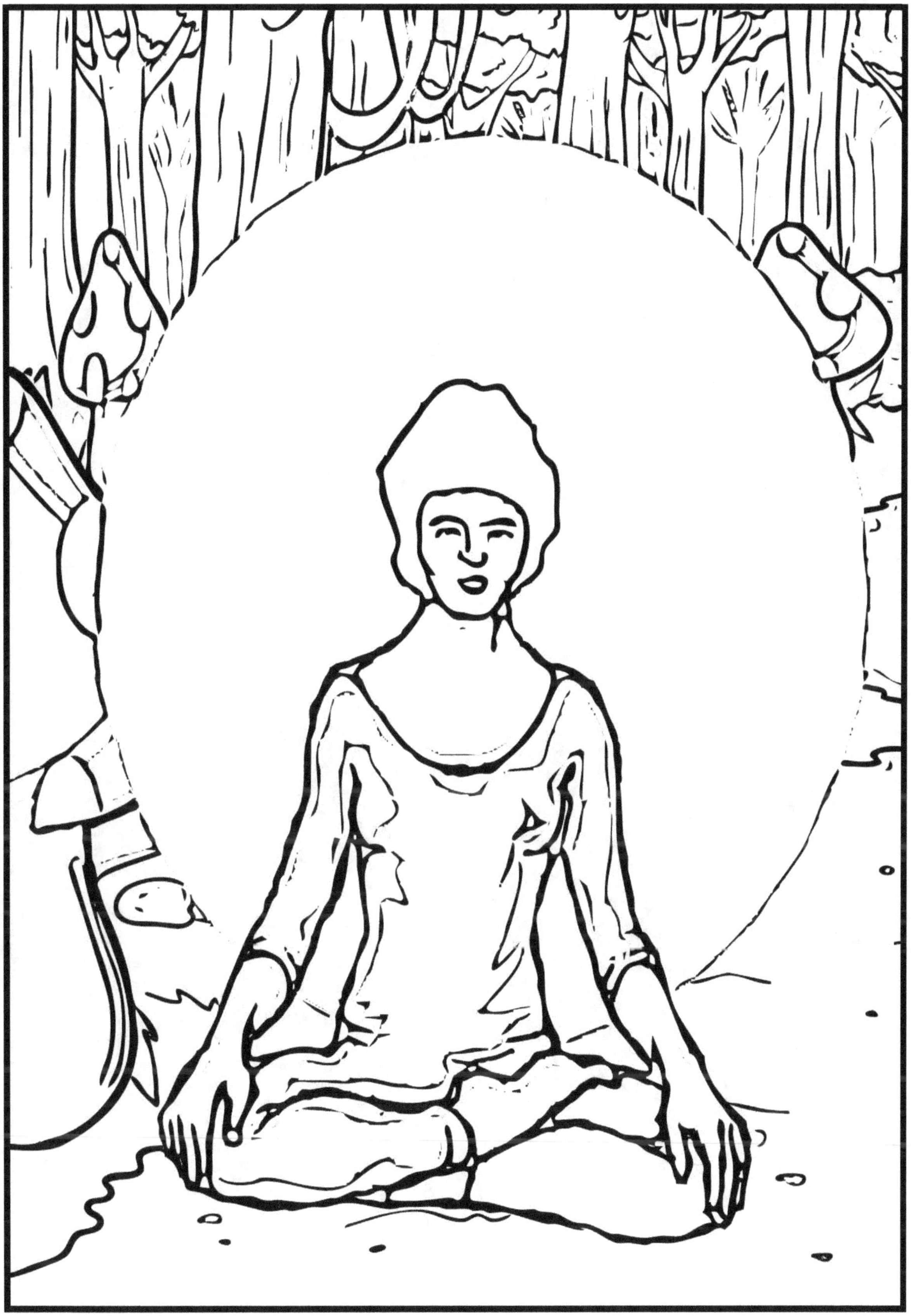

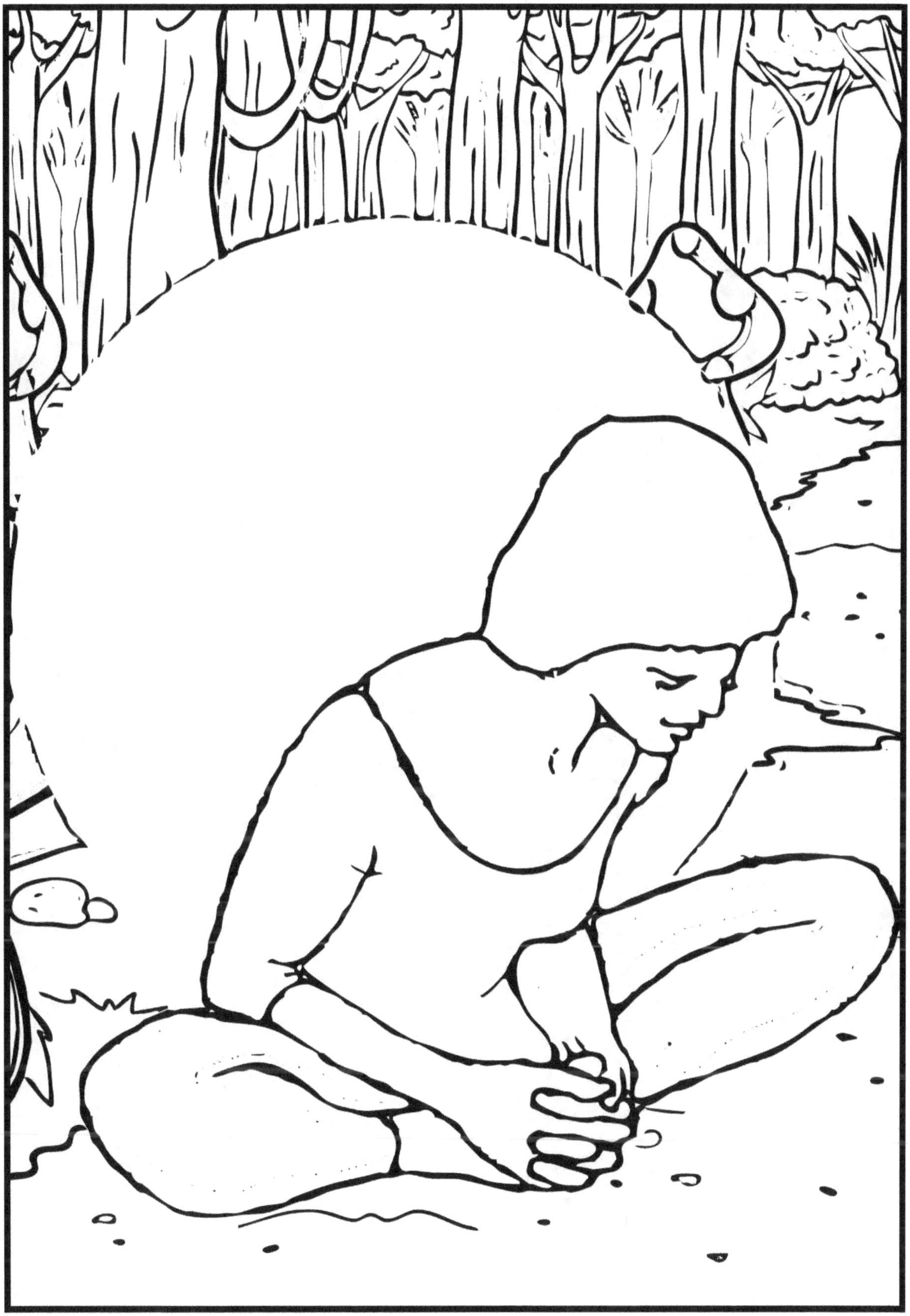

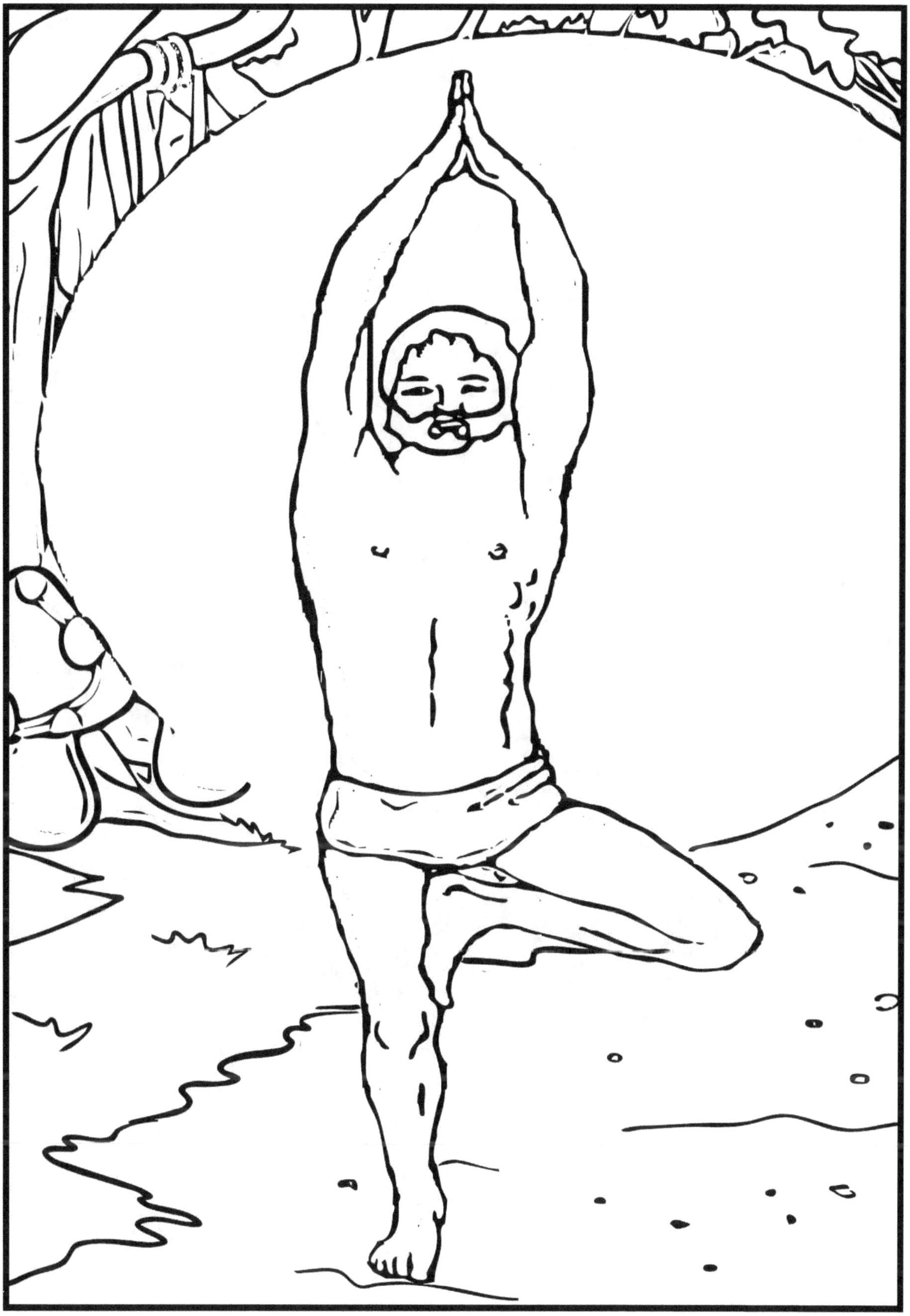

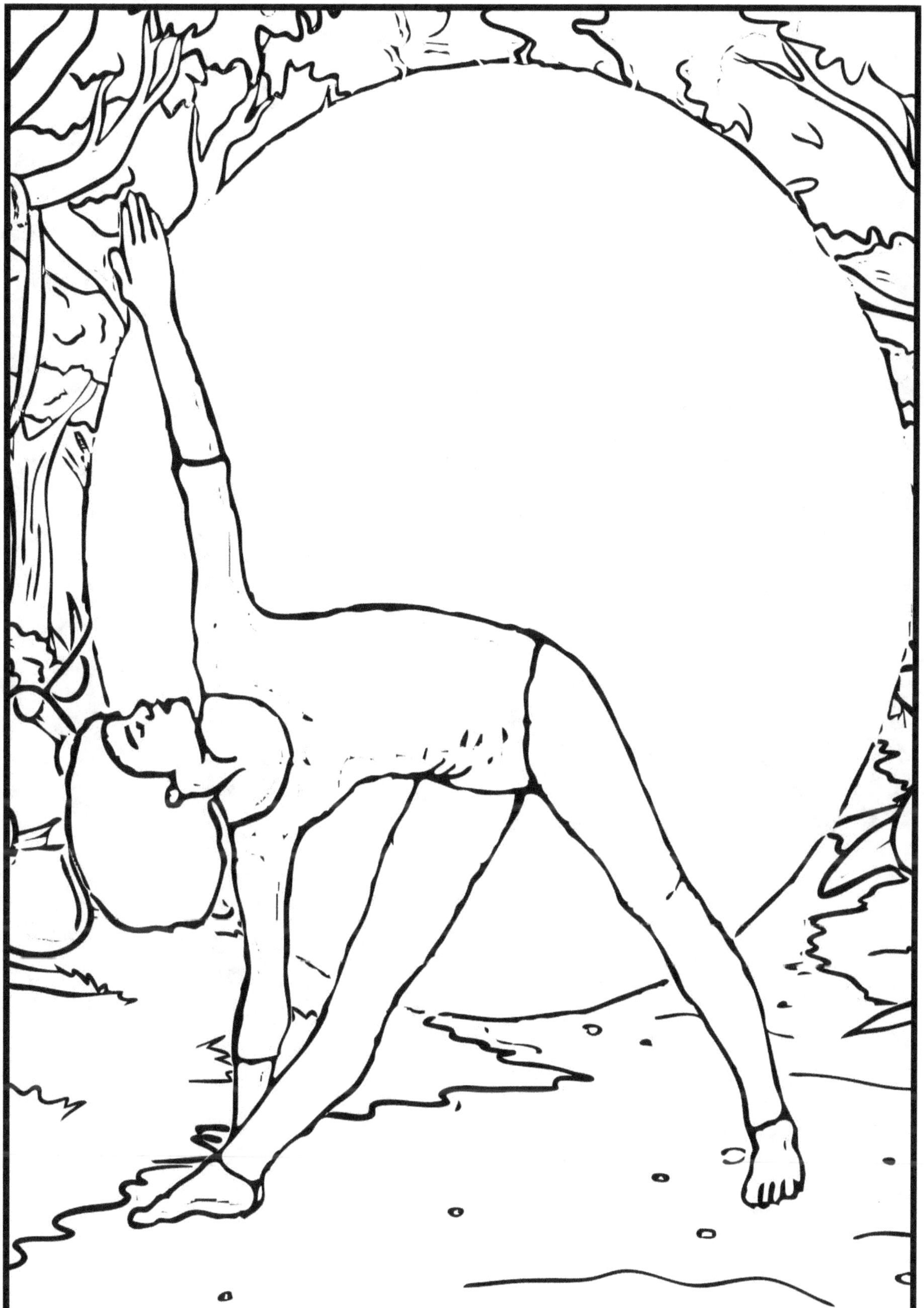

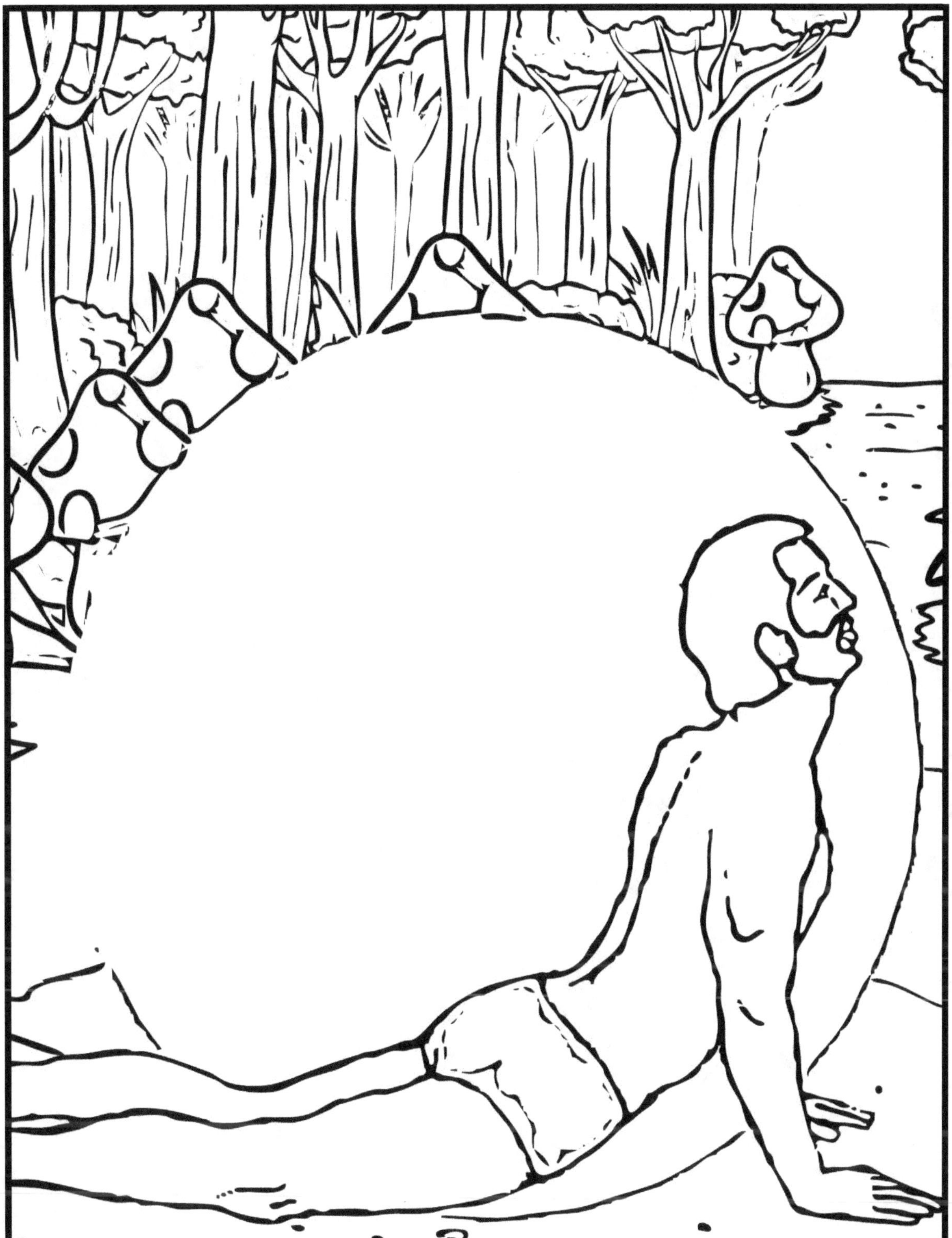

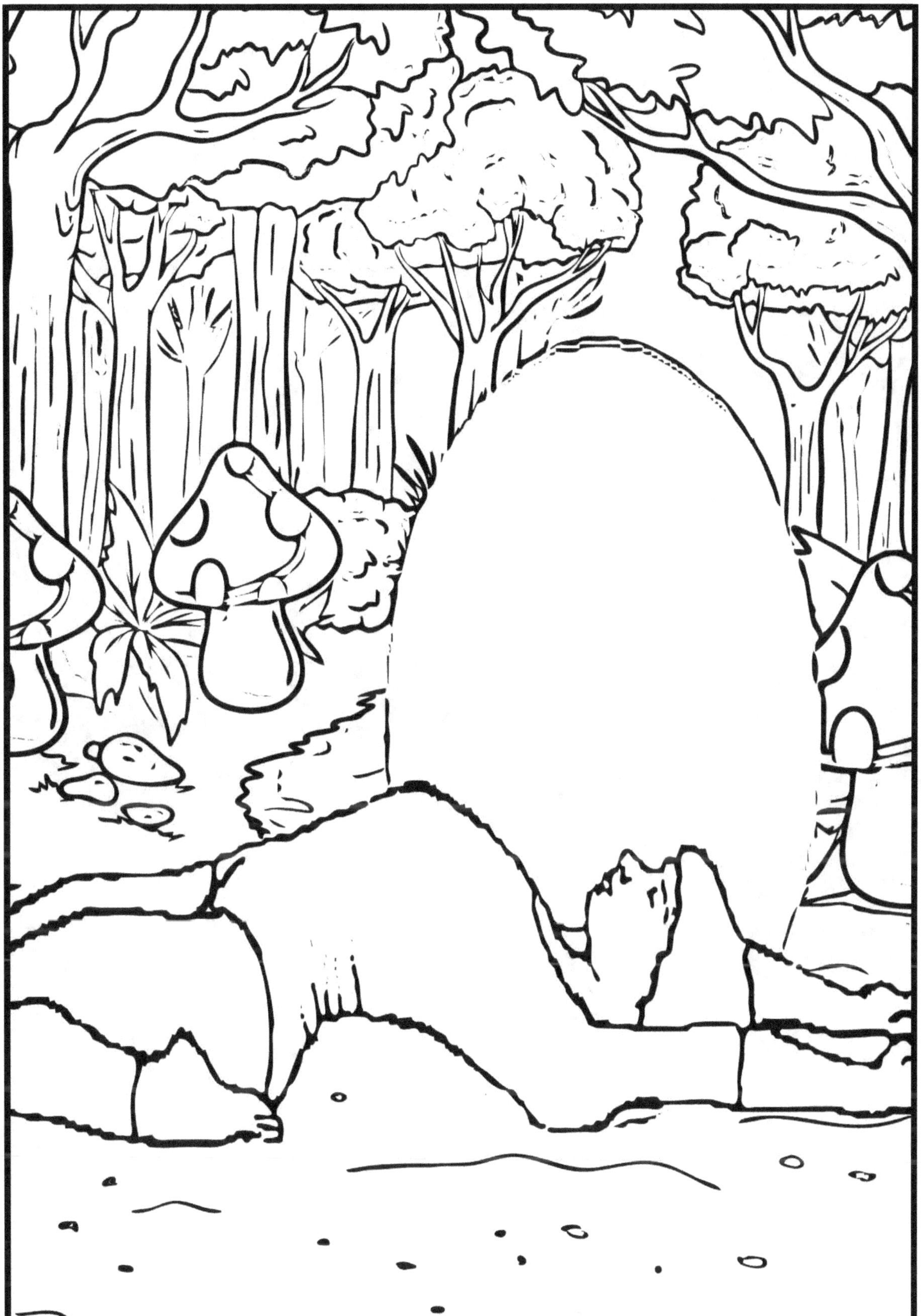

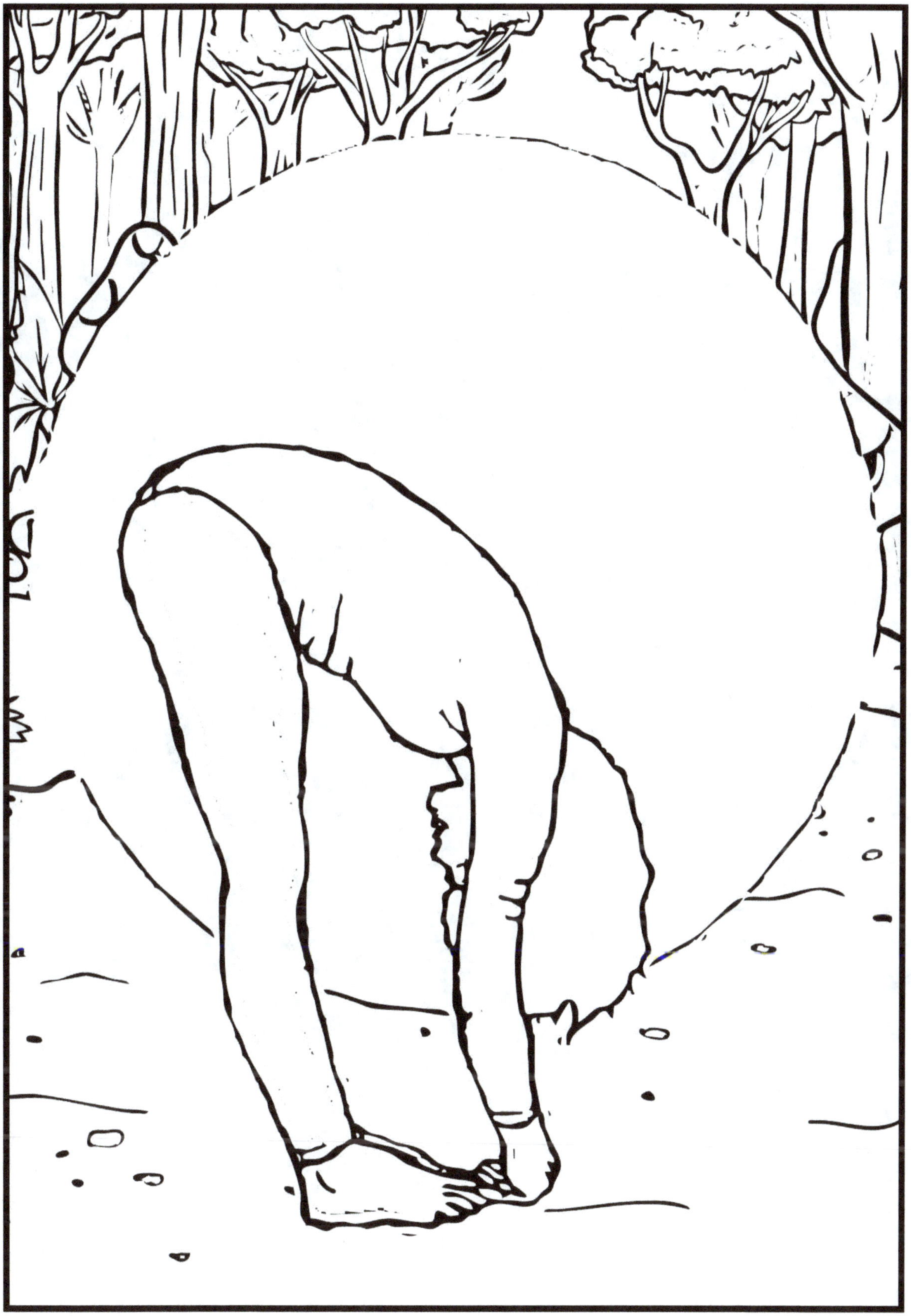

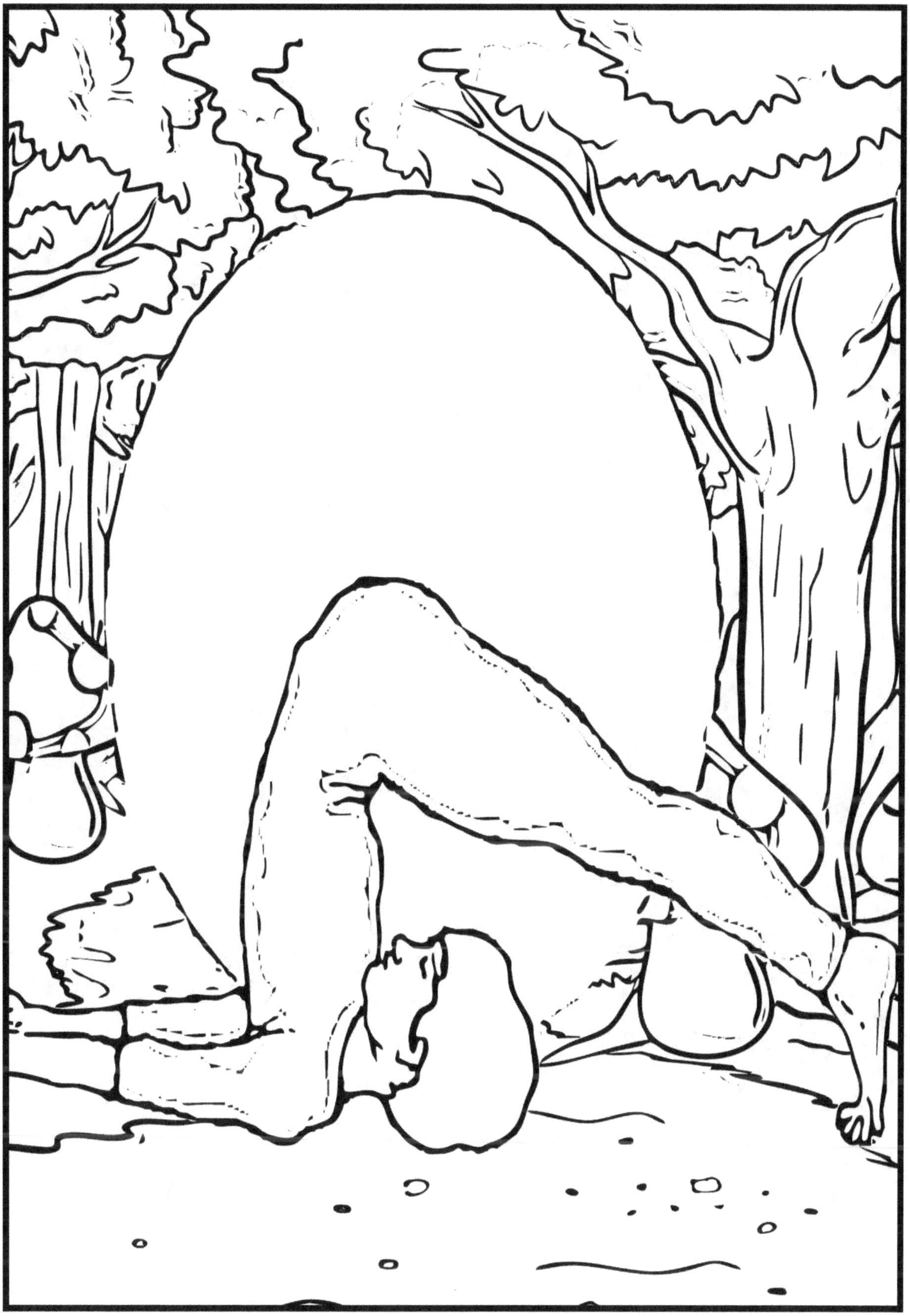

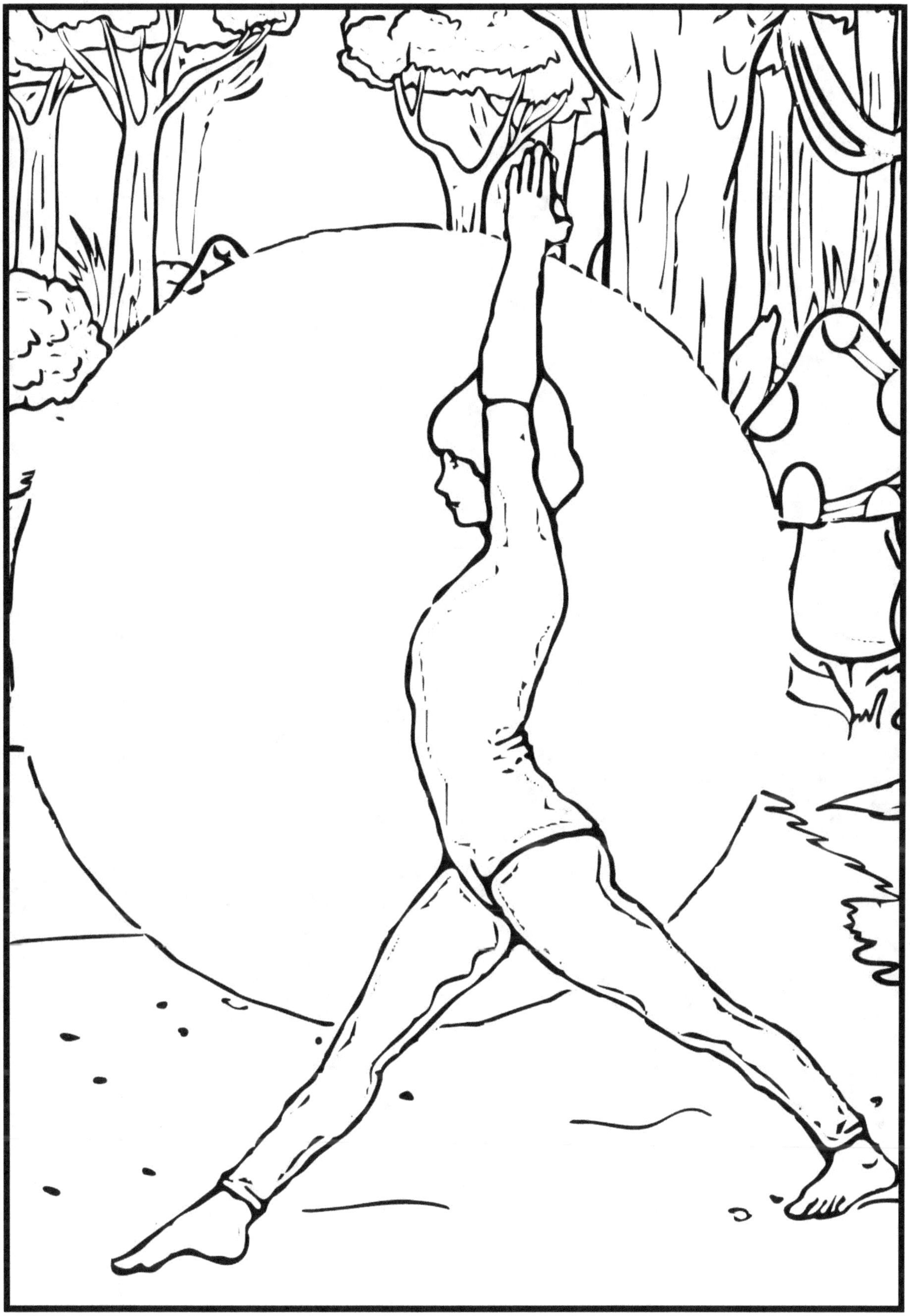

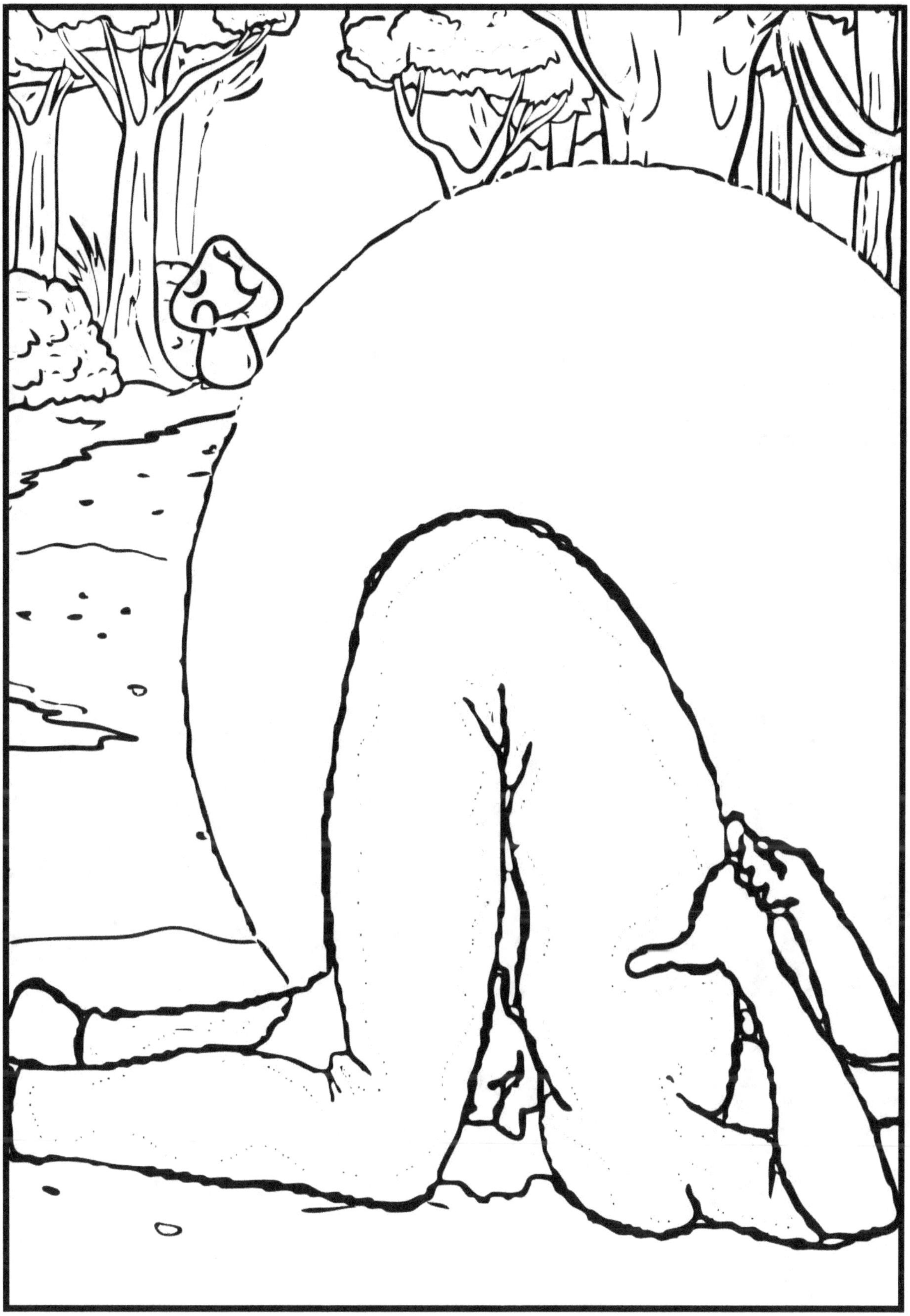

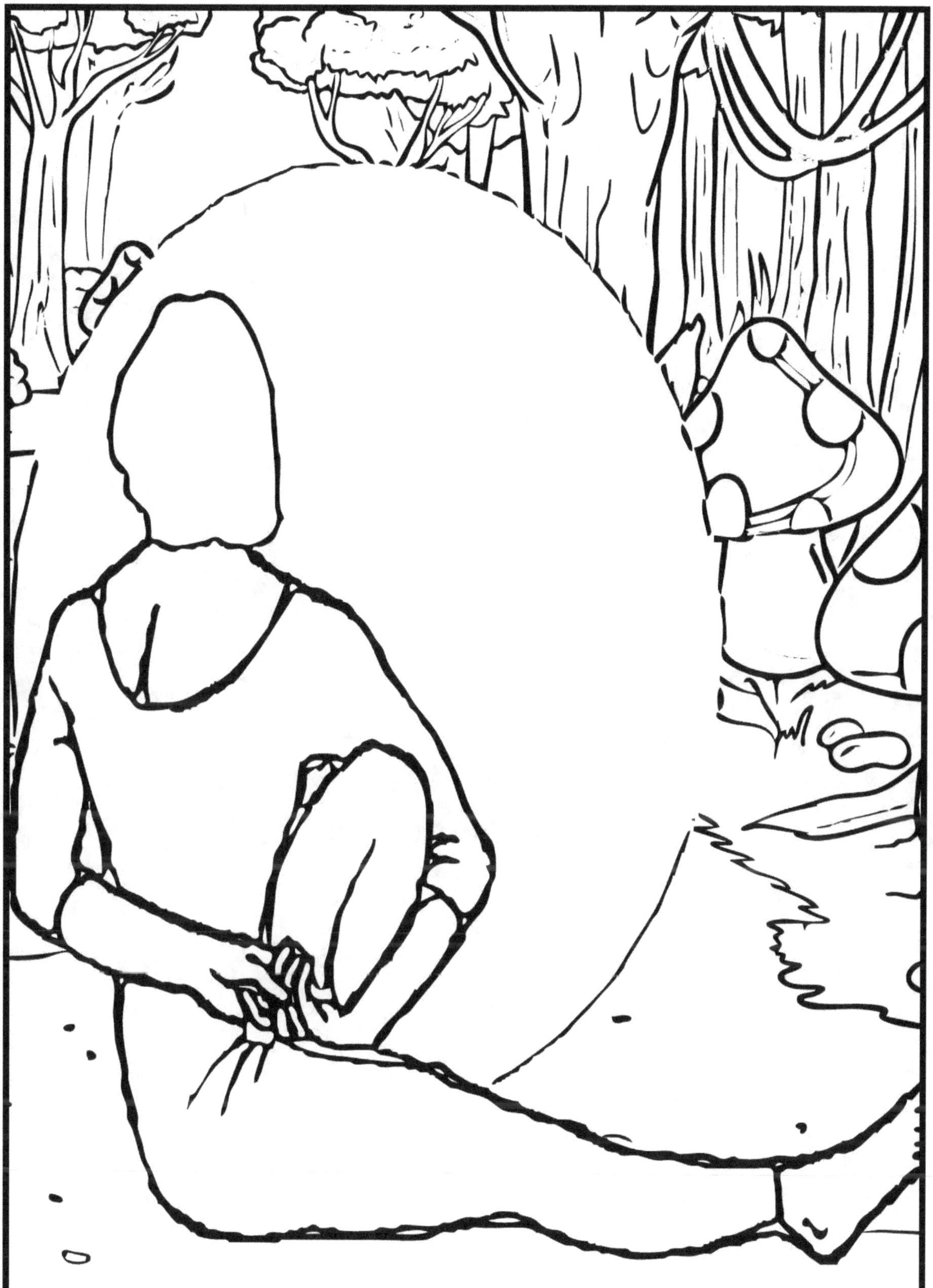

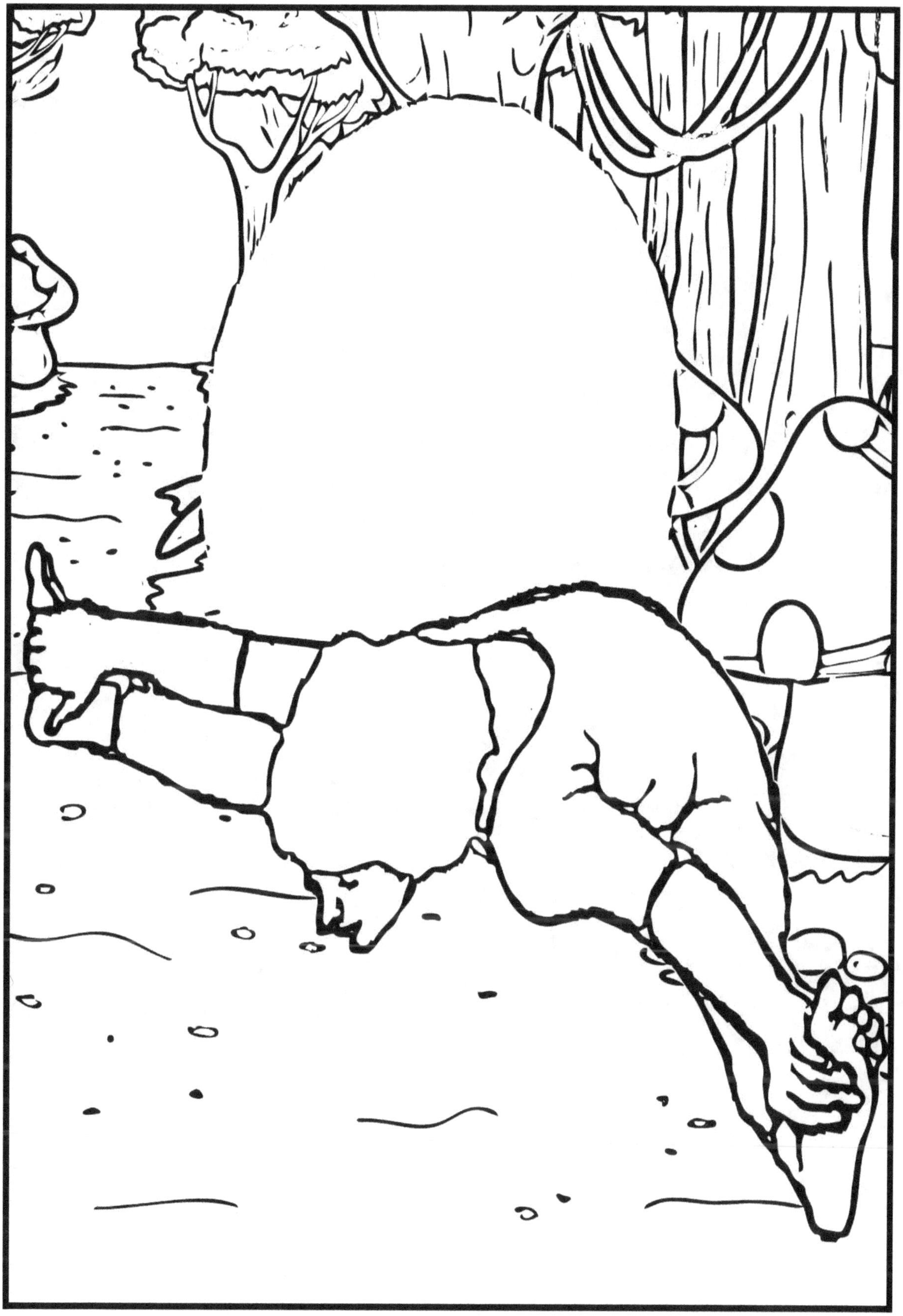

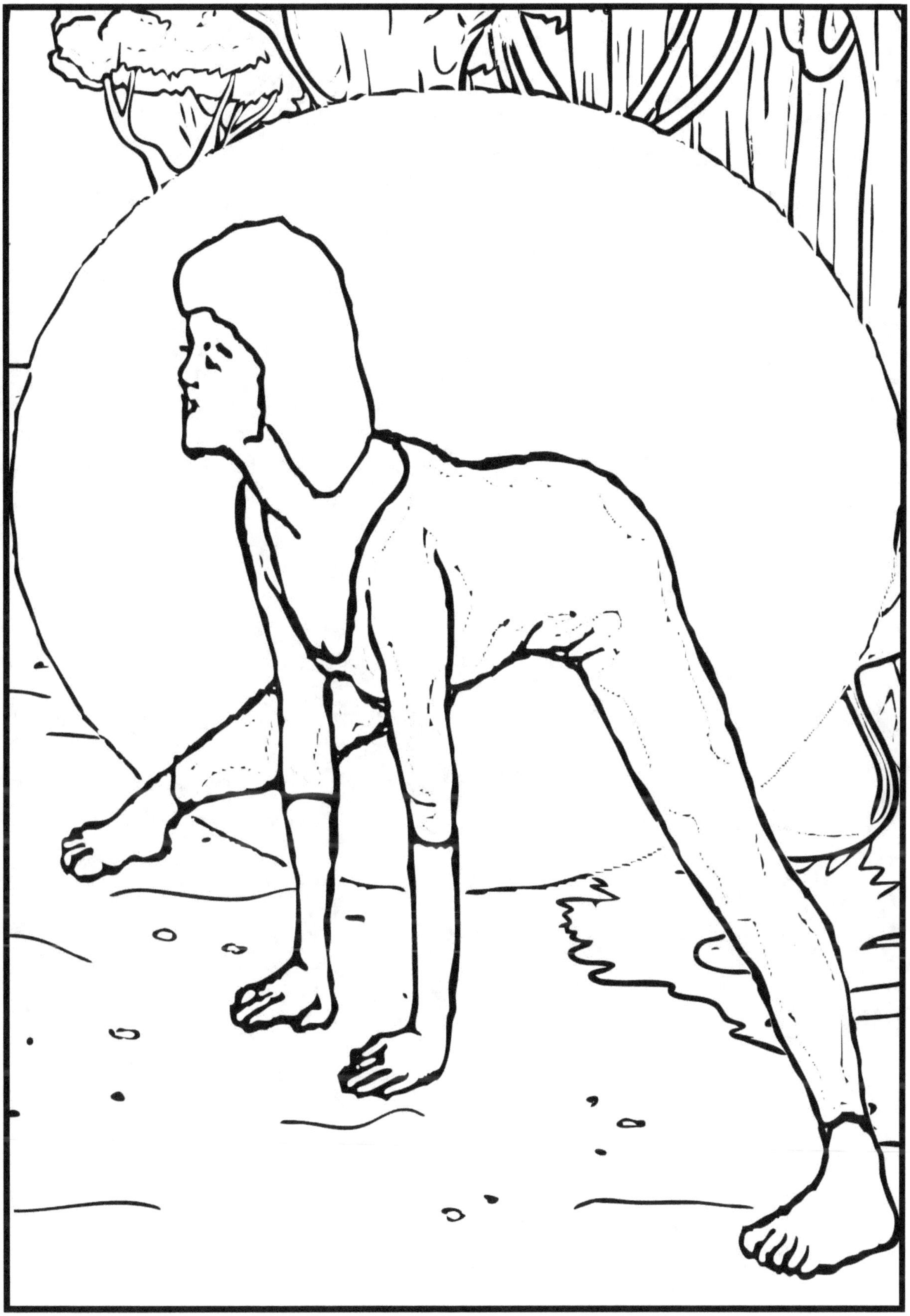

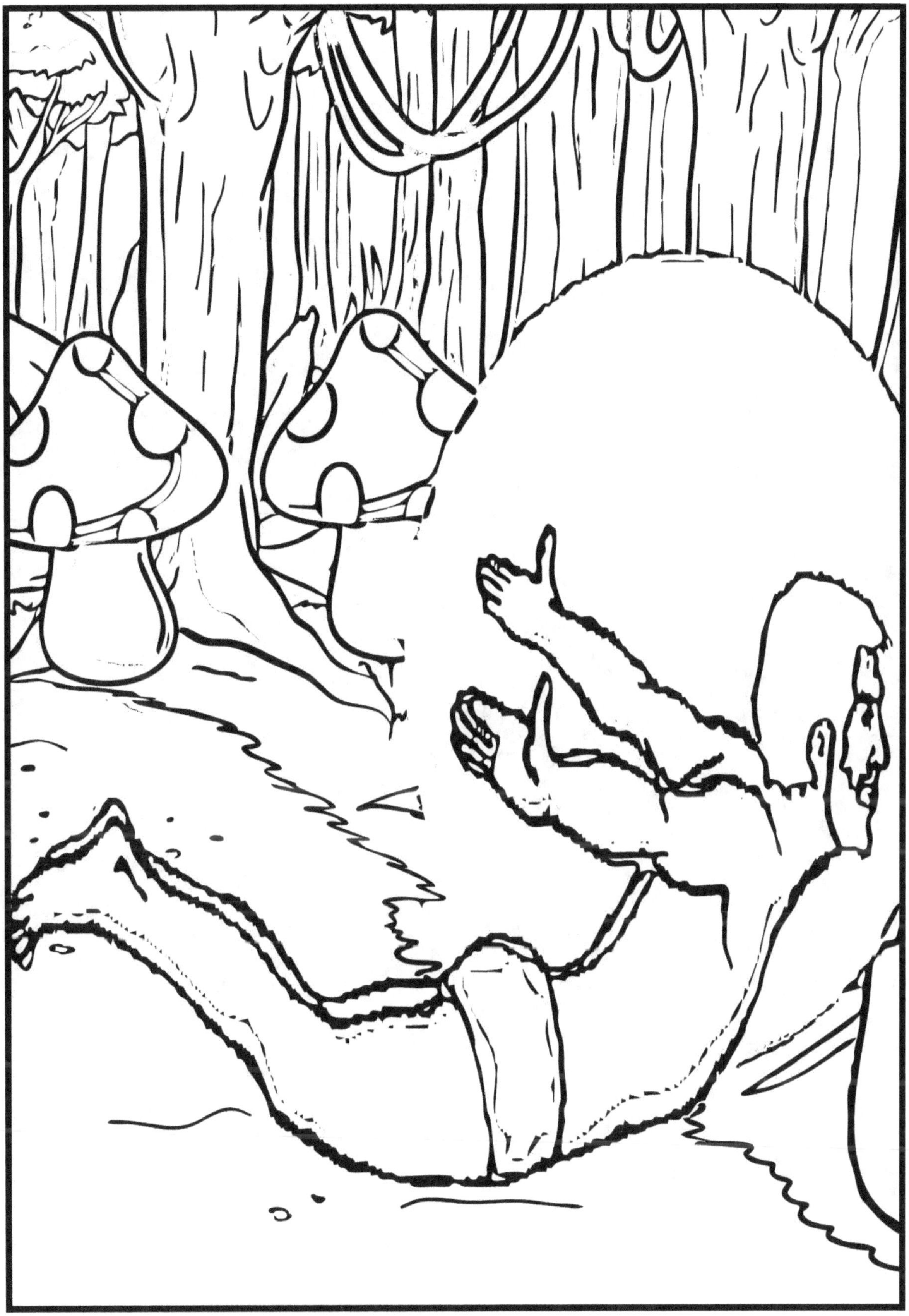

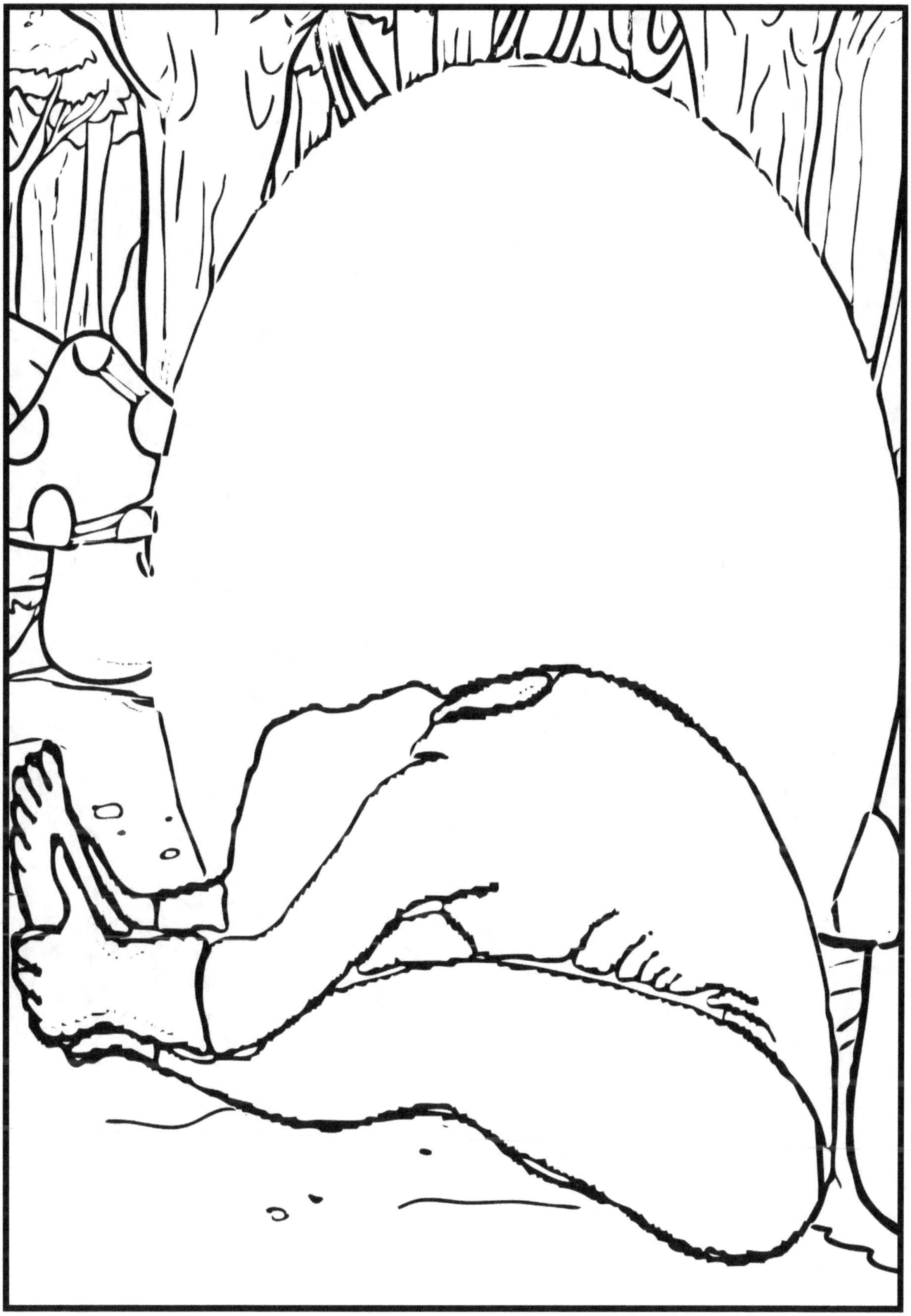

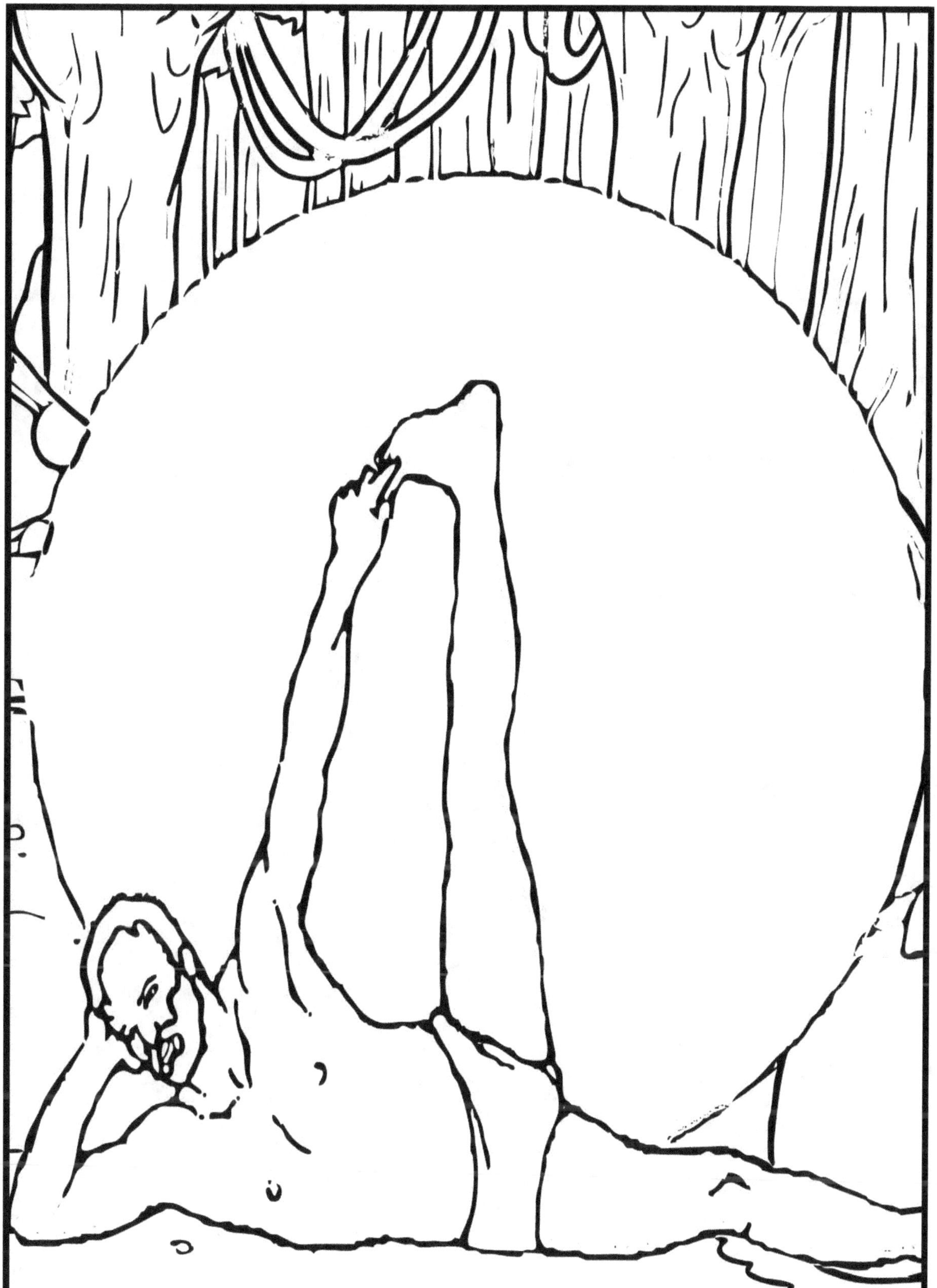

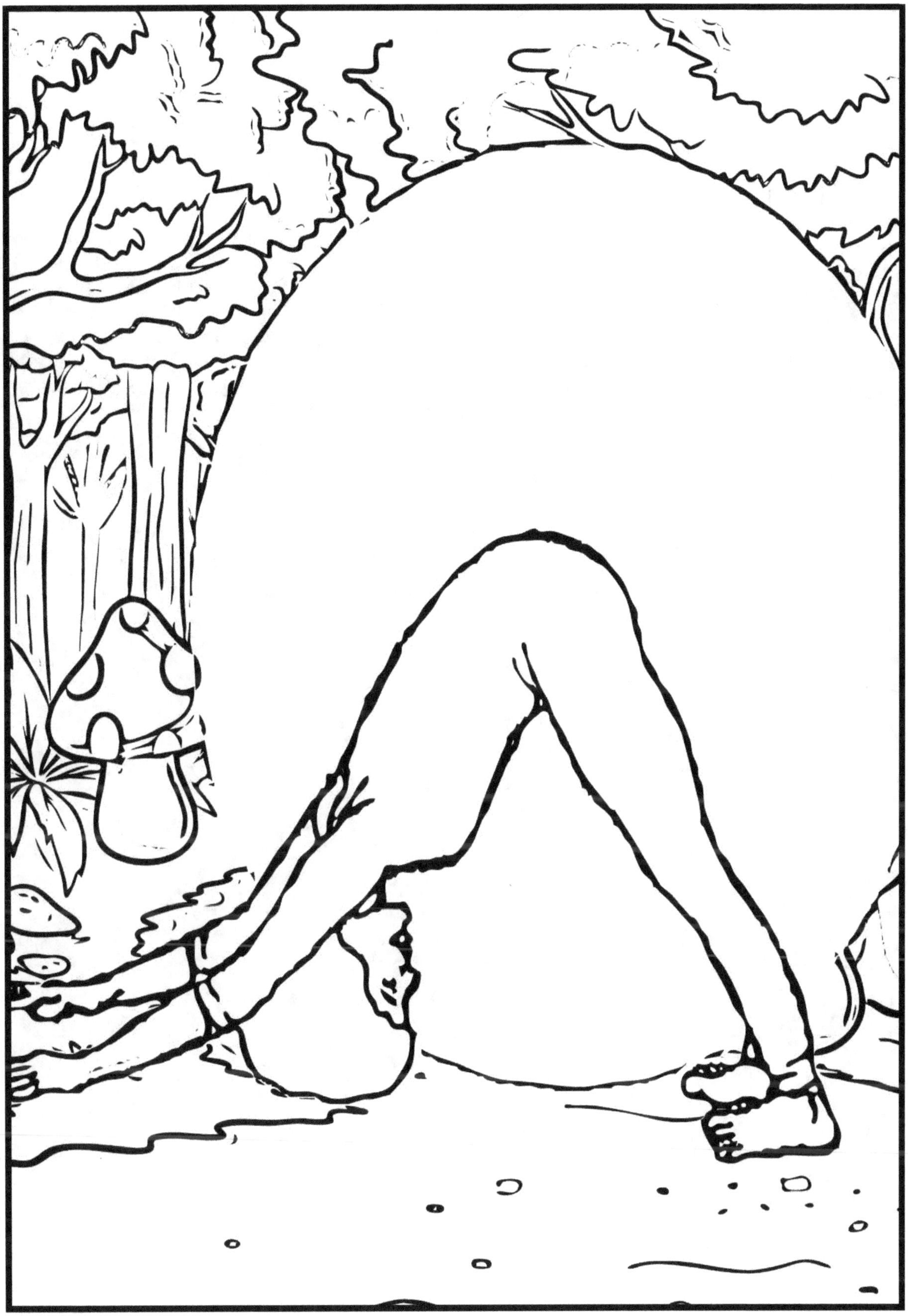

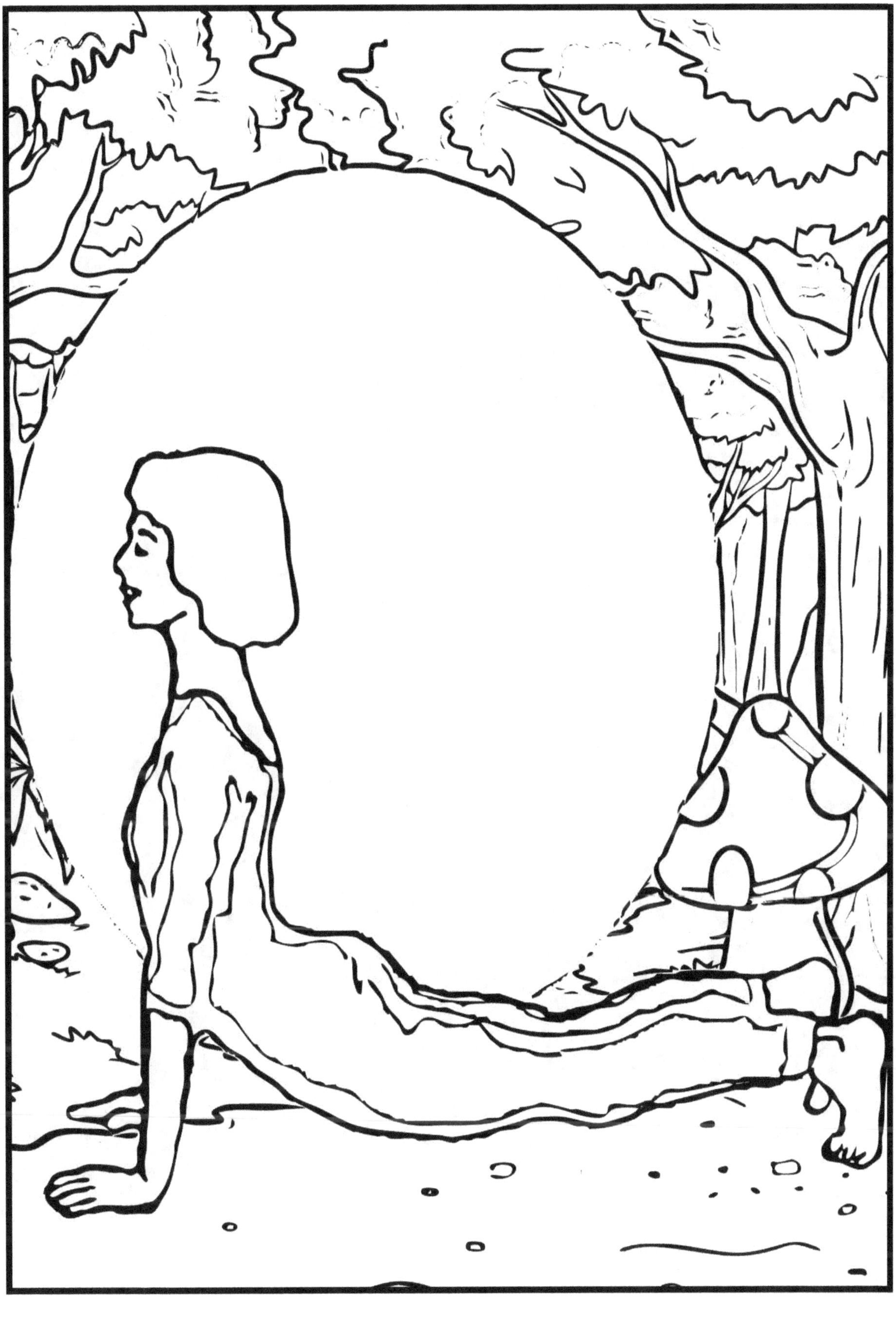

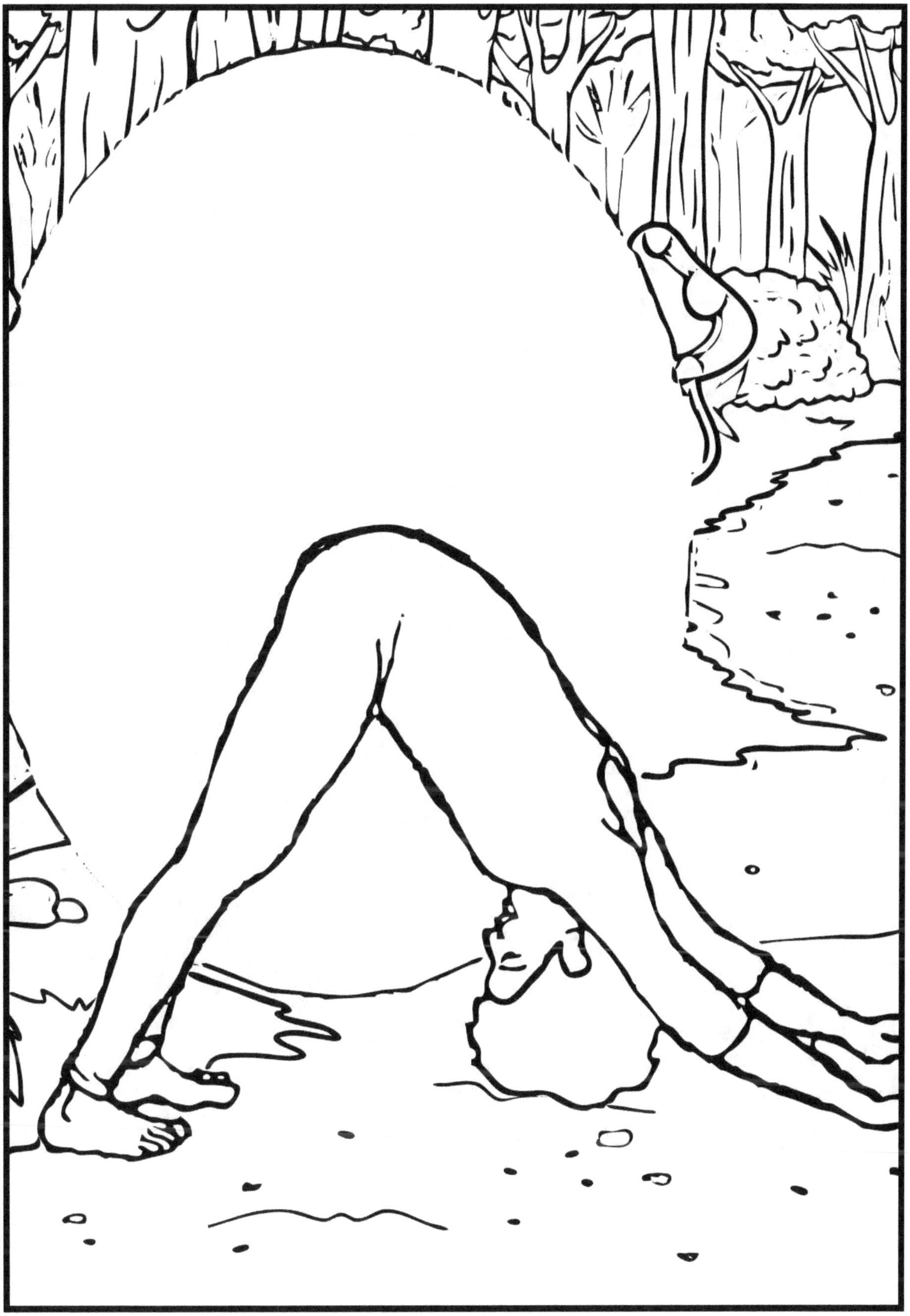

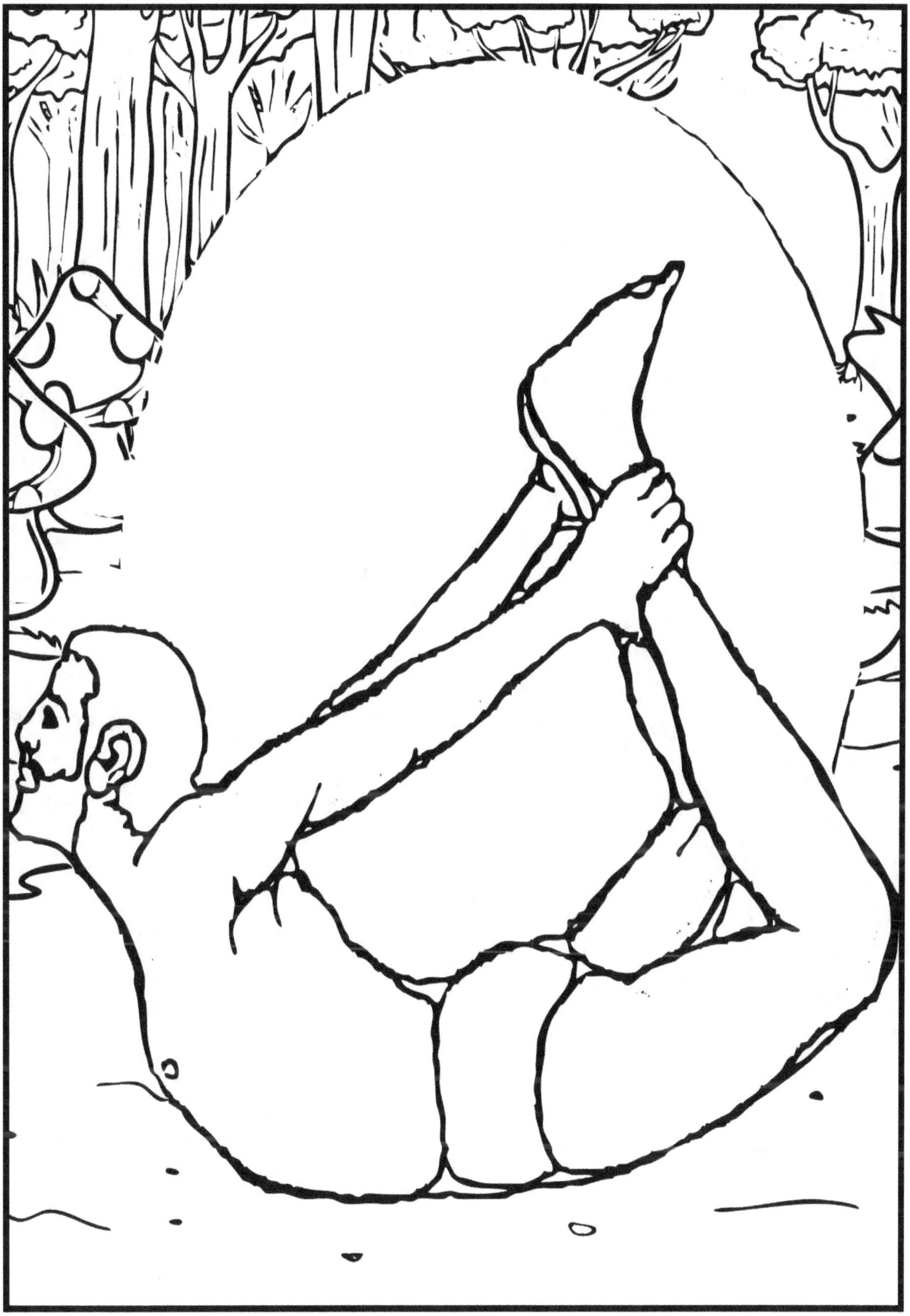

www.ingramcontent.com/pod-product-compliance
Lightning Source LLC
Chambersburg PA
CBHW081402170526
45166CB00010B/3172
* 9 7 8 1 5 1 9 6 3 0 3 0 8 *